THIS BOOK BELONGS TO

- -

- -

BONUS OFFER!!

Join Our Club And Get Free Bonus Pdf!

SIMPLY SEND US AN EMAIL TO:

BooksOfAllIntroductory@gmail.com

AND YOU WILL GET THE FOLLOWIG:

⋆ 10 Free Pages Of Pdf!
⋆ An Entry To Our Monthly Giveaway
Of $50 Amazon Gift

We Draw A New Winner Each Month And Will Contact Via Email

FOLLOW US

@booksofallintroductory

GOOD LUCK!!

Printed in Great Britain
by Amazon